Exploring SPACE A to Z

An ABC Book for Curious Kids with Interesting Facts about Space

Dylanna Press

Published by Dylanna Press an imprint of Dylanna Publishing, Inc.
Copyright © 2023 by Dylanna Press

All images used under license from shutterstock.com

Editor: Julie Grady

A  is for Astronaut

Did you know that astronauts get to live and work in space? They explore space and make incredible discoveries that help us better understand our universe. They wear special suits called spacesuits to keep them safe while they explore. They do important science experiments and take incredible pictures of Earth and the stars. Can you imagine eating, sleeping, and even exercising while floating? That's just a day in the life of an astronaut!

B is for Black Holes

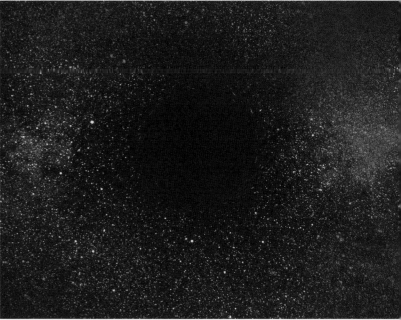

Imagine a vacuum cleaner so powerful that it can suck up everything around it, even light! That's what a black hole is like. They're made when a star runs out of fuel and collapses in on itself, creating an incredibly strong force called gravity that pulls everything nearby toward it. Black holes might be invisible, but scientists are like detectives, using clues to find them. They look for the way stars and gas nearby move and swirl, as if they're being pulled by an invisible force.

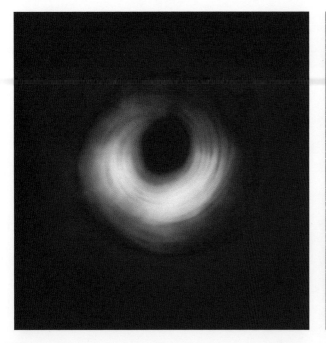

C is for Comets

Comets are like giant snowballs made of ice, dust, and gas. They come from the coldest, farthest regions of space, where everything is frozen and dark. When comets get closer to the sun, they start to melt and release gas, creating a beautiful tail that stretches across the sky. Sometimes, a comet gets close enough to Earth for us to see it in the night sky without a telescope. Have you ever seen a shooting star? That might have been a small piece of a comet burning up in the Earth's atmosphere! Keep an eye out at night, and you might just spot a comet's sparkling dance across the starry sky!

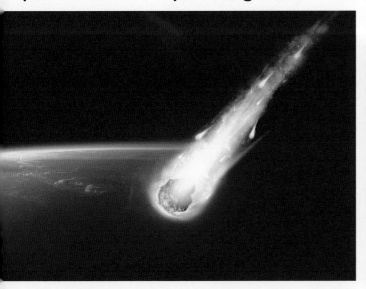

D is for Dwarf Planets

Dwarf planets are the cute little siblings of the big planets in our solar system! They're smaller than regular planets, but still love to twirl around the Sun in their own orbits. One famous dwarf planet, called Pluto used to be considered the ninth planet, but now we know it's actually a dwarf planet. Other dwarf planets are Ceres, Haumea, Makemake, and Eris. By studying dwarf planets, scientists hope to learn more about how our solar system formed and how these little worlds have changed over time.

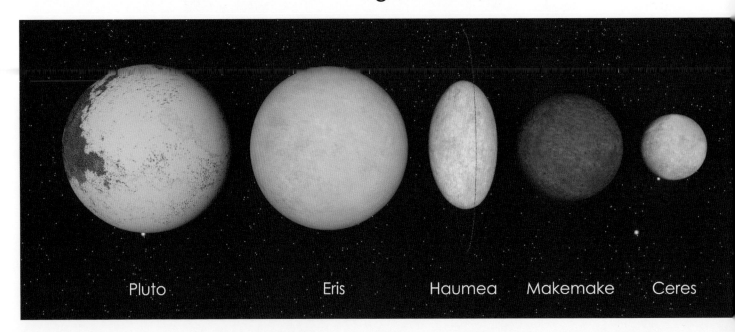

Pluto   Eris   Haumea   Makemake   Ceres

E is for Earth

Our home planet, Earth is like no other planet in our solar system. Earth is the third planet from the Sun, and it's the only planet we know of where life exists because it has just the right amount of air, water, and sunlight. It's like a giant, spinning ball made of rock and water, wrapped in a cozy, protective blanket called the atmosphere. This special layer of air keeps us warm, helps us breathe, and protects us from harmful rays and space rocks. Earth is our home and that's why it's important for us to take care of it!

F is for Falling Star

Falling stars, or shooting stars, are like magical wishes streaking across the night sky! They might look like stars tumbling from the sky, but they're actually tiny bits of dust and rock from space, called meteoroids, that zoom into Earth's atmosphere at super-fast speeds. As they speed along, they heat up and create a bright, glowing trail that looks like a star falling from the heavens. So, the next time you see a shooting star, make a wish and watch as it sparkles through the night!

G is for Galaxies

Galaxies are huge groups of stars that are held together by gravity. They come in all different shapes and sizes, and scientists believe there may be billions of them in the universe! The Milky Way is the galaxy that our solar system is part of, and it's home to over 100 billion stars. The Milky Way is shaped like a giant spiral, with graceful arms reaching out from a bright, glowing center. Looking up at the stars on a clear night can be a fun way to explore the galaxy right from your own backyard!

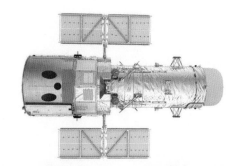

HUBBLE SPACE TELESCOPE

H is for Hubble Telescope

The Hubble Telescope is like a giant space camera that orbits Earth and takes amazing pictures of space! Launched into orbit in 1990, it helps us see into the farthest corners of the universe. It's named after the famous astronomer Edwin Hubble, who discovered that there were other galaxies besides our own. The Hubble can see things in space that are too far away for regular telescopes, and it's helped scientists make incredible discoveries about our universe. Thanks to the Hubble, we can explore the universe without ever leaving Earth!

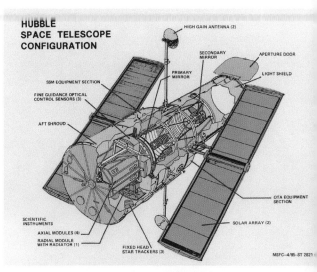

HUBBLE SPACE TELESCOPE CONFIGURATION

HIGH GAIN ANTENNA (2)

SECONDARY MIRROR

PRIMARY MIRROR

APERTURE DOOR

LIGHT SHIELD

SSM EQUIPMENT SECTION

FINE GUIDANCE OPTICAL CONTROL SENSORS (3)

AFT SHROUD

SCIENTIFIC INSTRUMENTS

AXIAL MODULES (4)

RADIAL MODULE WITH RADIATOR (1)

FIXED HEAD STAR TRACKERS (3)

OTA EQUIPMENT SECTION

SOLAR ARRAY (2)

MSFC–4/85-ST 2621

I is for International Space Station

The International Space Station is like a big house in space where astronauts live and work! It's the largest human-made object in space and orbits Earth about 250 miles above us. Astronauts from many different countries work there together, conducting experiments and learning about life in space. They even grow plants and exercise while floating around inside! The ISS is an amazing example of teamwork, proving that when we work together, we can achieve out-of-this-world things!

J  is for Jupiter

Jupiter is the giant king of our solar system, the largest of all the planets! Jupiter is the fifth planet from the Sun, and it's so big that it could fit more than 1,300 Earths inside it! This massive planet is made mostly of hydrogen and helium, the same gases that make up the Sun. It doesn't have a solid surface like Earth, but instead, it's like a giant, swirling ball of colorful clouds and storms. And, it has the most moons of any planet in our solar system—over 75!

K is for Kepler Telescope

The Kepler Telescope was launched in 2009 to search for new planets beyond our solar system. It's named after the famous scientist Johannes Kepler, who discovered that planets move in elliptical orbits around the sun. This amazing telescope has discovered thousands of new worlds called exoplanets. Thanks to Kepler, we now know that there are more planets in our galaxy than there are stars. That's a lot of planets! Kepler's discoveries have helped scientists learn about the incredible variety of worlds that exist in our galaxy, and have even given us clues about where we might find planets that could support life.

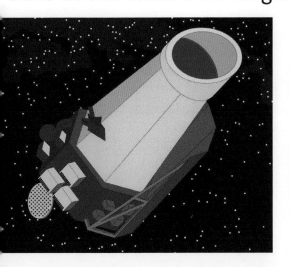

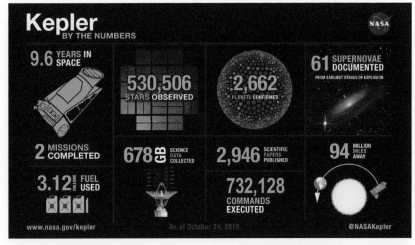

Kepler BY THE NUMBERS

9.6 YEARS IN SPACE

530,506 STARS OBSERVED

2,662 PLANETS CONFIRMED

61 SUPERNOVAE DOCUMENTED FROM EARLIEST STAGES OF EXPLOSION

2 MISSIONS COMPLETED

678 GB SCIENCE DATA COLLECTED

2,946 SCIENTIFIC PAPERS PUBLISHED

94 MILLION MILES AWAY

3.12 GALLONS FUEL USED

732,128 COMMANDS EXECUTED

www.nasa.gov/kepler   As of October 24, 2018   @NASAKepler

L is for Lunar Phases

Have you ever looked up at the night sky and noticed that the Moon looks different from one night to the next? Sometimes it's round and full, while other times it's just a thin, glowing crescent. These changing shapes of the Moon are called lunar phases. When the Moon is full, it looks like a giant ball in the sky. When it's a crescent, it looks like a smile! The lunar phases happen because of the way the sun's light reflects off the Moon. As the Moon orbits around Earth, different parts of its surface are lit up by sunlight, creating the different phases we see.

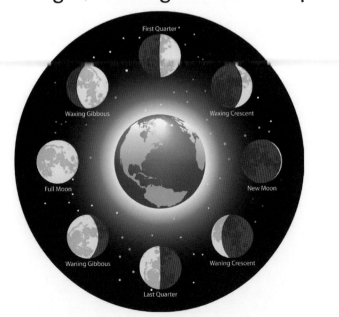

NEW MOON	WAXING CRESCENT	FIRST QUARTER	WAXING GIBBOUS

MOON PHASES

FULL MOON	WANING GIBBOUS	LAST QUARTER	WANING CRESCENT

M is for Moon

The Moon is Earth's closest cosmic buddy, lighting up our night sky with its gentle glow! It's covered in craters and mountains, and astronauts have even walked on its surface. The Moon always keeps one side facing us. That's why we always see the same pattern of craters and mountains on the Moon's surface, which some people think looks like a face, or the "Man in the Moon." The Moon has a very special role in our lives here on Earth. It affects the tides in our oceans, creates beautiful eclipses when it passes in front of the Sun, and its changing phases help us mark the passage of time.

N is for Nebulae

Nebulae are like cosmic nurseries where baby stars are born! Nebulae are made of clouds of gas and dust that float around in space. They come in all sorts of shapes, sizes, and colors, creating beautiful, glowing works of art in the sky. Nebulae are not only beautiful to look at, but they also teach us about the life cycle of stars and the incredible forces at work in our universe. They remind us that everything in space is connected, and that even as stars are born, grow, and eventually fade away, new stars are always being created.

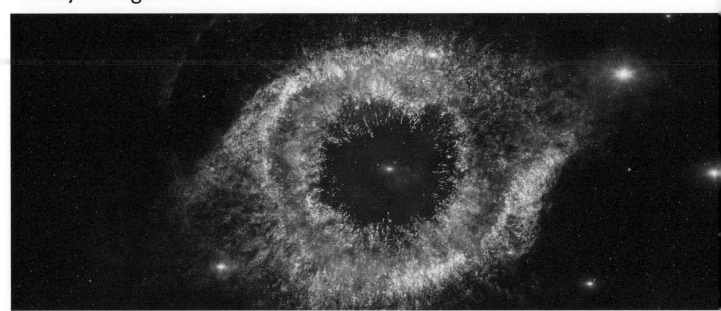

 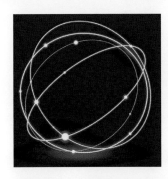 

is for Orbits

An orbit is the invisible path that objects in space follow as they travel around other objects, like Earth orbiting the Sun, or the Moon orbiting Earth. They follow these paths because of an invisible force called gravity that keeps them from flying off into space. This force keeps them from flying away and helps them follow their orbits. Earth takes a whole year to make one trip around the Sun and this journey through space is what gives us our seasons, like spring, summer, fall, and winter.

P

is for Planets

Planets are large cosmic objects that follow their own orbit around a star. In our solar system, there are eight amazing planets, including Earth, where we live. Some planets are giant balls of gas, like Jupiter, while others are rocky and have stunning landscapes, like Mars. They all have different colors, temperatures, and geographies that make them unique. These amazing worlds spin around the Sun, traveling together on an incredible journey through the universe.

is for Quasars

Quasars look like stars when seen through a telescope, but they're actually super bright centers of galaxies. Scientists believe that quasars are caused by massive black holes in the center of the galaxy, that are gobbling up lots of gas and dust. As the black hole eats, it creates a brilliant glow that can be seen from billions of light-years away. The light from quasars takes a very long time to travel across space and reach us here on Earth. Sometimes, it takes billions of years! That means when we look at a quasar, we are actually seeing what it looked like billions of years ago, like a cosmic time machine!

R is for Rockets

Rockets are powerful machines that can blast off from Earth, carrying astronauts, satellites, and even robots into space. They have engines that burn special fuel and create super-hot gases. These gases escape through a nozzle at the bottom of the rocket, creating a powerful force called thrust. This thrust pushes the rocket up into the sky. Rockets have to be designed just right to make sure they can withstand the intense heat and pressure of leaving Earth's atmosphere.

is for Stars

Stars are giant balls of gas that burn really hot and bright. Stars come in all different sizes, colors, and temperatures. The color of a star can tell us how hot or cool it is. Red stars are cooler, while blue stars are super-hot! Did you know that our very own Sun is actually a star? It's true! The Sun is a special kind of star called a yellow dwarf, and it's the closest star to Earth. In the night sky, stars make beautiful patterns called constellations.

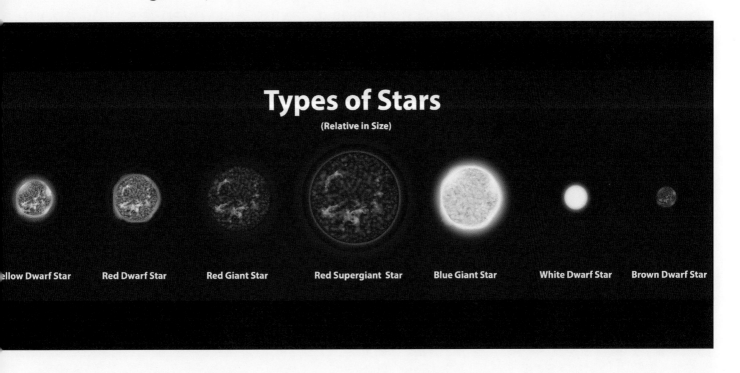

Types of Stars
(Relative in Size)

| Yellow Dwarf Star | Red Dwarf Star | Red Giant Star | Red Supergiant Star | Blue Giant Star | White Dwarf Star | Brown Dwarf Star |

T is for Telescopes

Telescopes let us see things in space that our eyes can't. They help us see planets, stars, and galaxies that are far, far away. Telescopes come in many sizes, from small ones that you can hold in your hand, to giant ones that are as big as a building! By collecting and focusing light, telescopes make far-away objects appear much closer, as if they were right in our own backyard. Telescopes have helped us make many amazing discoveries, like finding new planets, uncovering the secrets of distant galaxies, and even learning about the history of the universe itself!

U is for Universe

The universe is so big that even if you could travel at the speed of light, it would take you billions of years just to explore a tiny part of it! The universe began about 13.8 billion years ago, in a spectacular event called the Big Bang. This incredible explosion created all the matter, energy, and even time itself, setting the stage for the magnificent cosmos we see today. Our universe is home to countless amazing sights like stars, galaxies, planets, and so much more. In this vast universe, our home, the Milky Way galaxy, is just one of billions of galaxies, each filled with billions of stars. And our little solar system, with our Sun and its family of planets, is just a small neighborhood within the Milky Way.

V is for Venus

Venus is Earth's neighbor and is about the same size with a similar rocky surface. But Venus is way too hot to live on, because it has a thick atmosphere, made mostly of carbon dioxide, that traps in heat. It's the hottest planet in our solar system with a surface temperature hot enough to melt lead, reaching up to 900 degrees Fahrenheit (475 degrees Celsius)! This dazzling world shines so brightly in the sky that it's sometimes mistaken for a star! Sometimes, it's even called the "morning star" or the "evening star" because of its stunning glow.

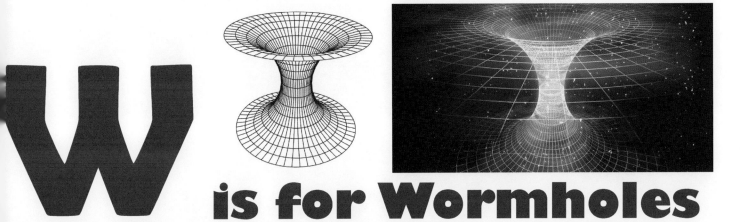

W is for Wormholes

Wormholes are like secret space tunnels that might connect different parts of the universe! Imagine sliding through a twisty cosmic straw to travel great distances in the blink of an eye. Scientists believe that wormholes might be possible, but they're hard to find and even harder to travel through. Even though we haven't found any real wormholes yet, scientists love to imagine what they could be like and how they might work.

X is for X-ray Astronomy

Just like doctors use X-rays to peek inside our bodies, astronomers use X-ray telescopes to explore things we can't see with our eyes alone. These special telescopes help us study stars, galaxies, and black holes that are too far away to see with regular telescopes. By studying the x-rays coming from these objects, astronomers can learn things they couldn't before. X-ray astronomy can even help us find out what's inside places like old supernova explosions to better understand our universe!

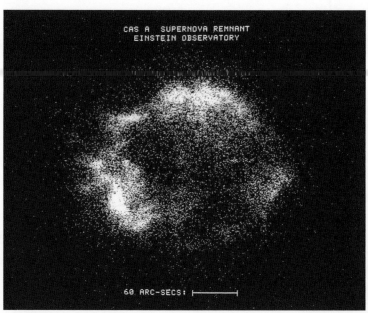

Y is for Yellow Dwarf

Yellow dwarfs are medium-sized stars, including our very own Sun, that shine with a warm, yellow light. They're not too hot and not too cold, which makes them perfect for sustaining life on planets orbiting around them. Yellow dwarf stars, like our Sun, are middle-aged stars in their life cycle and they can live for a very long time, up to 10 billion years. But don't be fooled by the name "dwarf"—yellow dwarf stars are actually quite large. Our Sun, for example, is so big that you could fit more than a million Earths inside it!

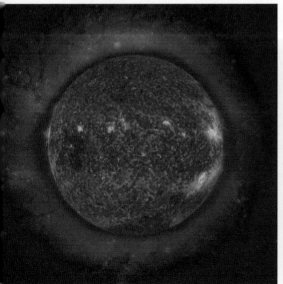

Z is for Zodiac Constellations

The zodiac constellations are a fascinating part of the night sky—they have been used by people throughout history to track the seasons and create calendars. There are 12 zodiac constellations, and each is connected to a specific time of the year. As the Earth orbits the Sun, different constellations appear in the sky during different months. For example, Aries the Ram can be seen in April, Leo the Lion in August, and Scorpio the Scorpion in November. So, the next time you gaze up at the night sky, try to spot the zodiac constellations and imagine the incredible stories they hold!

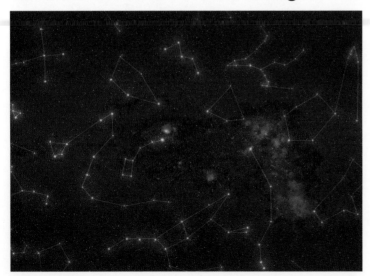

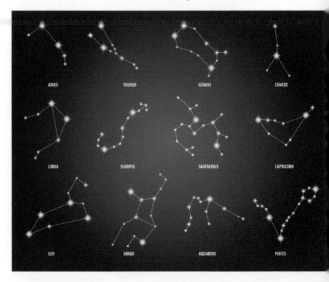

Printed in Great Britain
by Amazon